A STUDENT'S GUIDE TO
LIBERAL LEARNING

THE PRESTON A. WELLS JR.

GUIDES TO THE MAJOR DISCIPLINES

GENERAL EDITOR   EDITOR

JEFFREY O. NELSON   JEREMY BEER

PHILOSOPHY *Ralph M. McInerny*

LITERATURE *R. V. Young*

LIBERAL LEARNING *James V. Schall, S.J.*

THE STUDY OF HISTORY *John Lukacs*

THE CORE CURRICULUM *Mark C. Henrie*

U.S. HISTORY *Wilfred M. McClay*

ECONOMICS *Paul Heyne*

POLITICAL PHILOSOPHY *Harvey C. Mansfield*

PSYCHOLOGY *Daniel N. Robinson*

CLASSICS *Bruce S. Thornton*

AMERICAN POLITICAL THOUGHT *George W. Carey*

RELIGIOUS STUDIES *D. G. Hart*

A Student's Guide to Liberal Learning

JAMES V. SCHALL, S.J.

ISI BOOKS
WILMINGTON, DELAWARE

For further essays, educational resources, and guidance from James V. Schall, visit his website at www.moreC.com/schall.

The Student Self-Reliance Project and the ISI Guides to the Major Disciplines are made possible by grants from the Philip M. McKenna Foundation, the Wilbur Foundation, F. M. Kirby Foundation, Castle Rock Foundation, the people of MBNA America, and other contributors who wish to remain anonymous. The Intercollegiate Studies Institute gratefully acknowledges their support.

Copyright © 2000 Intercollegiate Studies Institute
Fourth printing, February 2006

Cataloging-in-Publication Data

Schall, James V.
     A student's guide to liberal learning / by James V. Schall.
     2nd ed.—Wilmington, Del. : ISI Books, 2000.

     p. cm.

     ISBN 1-882926-53-6
     1. Education, Humanistic. 2. Education — philosophy.
   I. Title. II. Title: Guide to liberal learning.

LC1011 .S33 2000   00-101234
370.11/2—dc21   CIP

Published in the United States by:

   ISI Books
   Post Office Box 4431
   Wilmington, DE 19807-0431

Cover and interior design by Sam Torode
Manufactured in the United States of America

CONTENTS

INTRODUCTORY NOTE

THE IMPORTANT THINGS, Aristotle told us, are to be known "for their own sakes," not for some useful or pleasurable purpose, however useful or pleasurable they might also be. Scholars tell us that the ages have saved for us Plato's literary works and Aristotle's more pedestrian class-notes or lectures. The first sing; the second demand our careful, repeated attention. The fact that we have both sorts of heritage contains a lesson for us. We oftentimes need to be called out of ourselves by something that is simply charming or delightful. At other times, we recognize that if we are to grasp the essence of something, it will take our undivided attention over a long period of time, perhaps a lifetime.

Where might we go, what might we do to find the truth, to find what makes sense, what incites us to use that mind we all have been given to pursue by it our human task, to know *what is*, to know what we ought to do? No age has an easy time of it, trying to figure things out. Our age has difficulty asking these questions, not merely because we have so much knowledge available to us or because, compared with other ages, there are so many of us, but also because we are an age of doubt, an age that does not seem to want to know what it can know.

The human mind must also choose to use itself properly to achieve its primary purpose which is to find the truth of things. When a human being is functioning normally, when he is being what he is given by nature to be, he is using his mind. And yet, the mind can talk itself out of using itself. Many great thinkers suspect this choice is what has happened to us. We have talked ourselves out of knowing what we can know, and in particular, what we are.

Is there anything we might do about this? What we need to do is to find some guide, some book, some friend, some professor perhaps, some lecture, some journal or essay, that will alert us to the fact that what we are mostly given is skewed. This discovery will not be easy. We do not like to rethink things. We do not like to challenge commitments to schools or faculty or ideas that bear the mark of popularity or accepted habit.

Many doubt and are taught to doubt whether things can, in principle, be true. Indeed, few are allowed to think, as a first premise, anything else but doubt and are surprised, on examination, at the little evidence there is for such a position. Where does this situation leave the bewildered student, the potential philosopher, as Plato called him? It leaves him largely on his own, or at least at first sight. This essay is addressed primarily to those present and former students at college, university, and graduate levels, and their parents, who are aware that what is being presented to them in the classroom has something seriously skewed about it. But this essay is *not* an anti-intellectual tractate— just the opposite. It is designed to alert the inquiring student to the fact that, as the famous philosopher Etienne Gilson once wrote in his remarkable *The Unity of Philosophical Experience*, "there are things and I can know them." This essay is a guide to true liberal education, one that is capable of alerting us to intellectual riches that are almost never found in universities or in the popular culture.

So what one reads here is after the manner of a minority opinion. I will be enthusiastic about books, authors, and ideas about which most students will never have heard or, having heard of them, will have heard nothing good about them. Thinking is itself, however, an adventure. If some-one wants to begin, he could do worse than to begin with the books and ideas that I have indicated here. Needless to say, this guide to "liberal learning," as it is called, is not extensive. Yet, each book read leads to something else. I dare say, that by the time a student has pursued ideas in the first book he finds mentioned here, he will be in that profound period of life Cicero called "old age," the title of one of his essays that I want everyone who begins these reflections eventually to read, preferably before old age itself.

I WOULD NOT represent [Robert E.] Lee as a prophet, but as a man who stood close enough to the eternal verities to utter prophecy sometimes when he spoke. He was brought up in the old school, which places responsibility upon the individual, and not upon some abstract social agency. Sentimental humanitarianism manifestly does not speak to language of duty, but of indulgence. The notion that obligations are tyrannies, and that wants, not deserts, should be the measure of what one gets has by now shown its destructive power. We have tended to ignore the inexorable truth that rights must be earned. Fully interpreted, Lee's "duty" is the measure whereby freedom preserves itself by acknowledging responsibility. Man, then, perfects himself by discipline, and at the heart of discipline lies self-denial. When the young mother brought an infant for Lee to bless, and was told, "Teach him to deny himself," she was receiving perhaps the deepest insight of his life.

—RICHARD WEAVER, "Lee as a Philosopher,"
The Southern Essays of Richard Weaver

FROM WHENCE DID THESE
OBSERVATIONS COME?

❧

BACK IN 1988, I wrote a book entitled *Another Sort of Learning.* The book was addressed to those students and ex-students who are quite aware that something is radically incomplete and wrong with formal higher education but are not quite sure why or what to do about it. The following was the none-too-pithy, somewhat brash subtitle: "*How Finally to Acquire an Education While Still in College or Anywhere Else, Containing Some Belated Advice about How to Employ Your Leisure Time When Ultimate Questions Remain Perplexing in Spite of Your Highest Earned Academic Degree, Together with Sundry Book Lists Nowhere Else in Captivity to Be Found.*" That subtitle, I confess, even though I wrote it, has always amused me. It set the stage for exactly what I wanted to say, while, at the same time, preserving some of the winsome spirit in which I wanted to say it.

That lengthy subtitle addresses the condition of soul in which many, if not most, students and variously aging ex-students and professors find themselves in today's social climate. Something fundamental has been missed. A sense of intellectual loss or confusion is especially acute in the so-called prestige and most expensive schools, but it occurs almost everywhere in academia.

Here I will try to recount something of what I said in *Another Sort of Learning*, but the fuller discussion of what I recommend to students remains to be found in that original book with the long subtitle. The main words of its title, "another sort of learning," hint at a vast wisdom that is exciting and available if we only knew how to go about finding it.

In *Another Sort of Learning*, moreover, were found chapters on sports, personal libraries, grades, reading, intellectual life, lectures, teaching, evil, and devotion, all of which, however odd it may seem, are related to the pursuit and acceptance of the truth. Too, along with these topics, can be found "*Schall's Unlikely List of Books to Keep Sane By*"—a list that I will reproduce at the end of this essay, with some new additions more recently found. Scattered throughout this particular essay, I will include brief lists of books on a given topic or by a given author. These will be items that I think are particularly pertinent and insightful, indeed often stirring, in the pursuit of the goal that I have mainly in mind for this essay on what must be called "an intellectual life open to the truth."

The present account will take a counter-cultural position and hint that something really different is around and is worth taking a look at if we can only find it. No one should be afraid of using his mind, or as Bertie Wooster of P. G. Wodehouse fame used to say, of using his "old bean." Wodehouse, by the way, I recommend to any one at all interested in how sanity and wit belong together. Our intellectual faculties were given to us precisely to use, to use correctly.

Three of the More Than One-hundred P. G. Wodehouse Novels: 1) *Leave It to Psmith,* 2) *Blandings Castle and Elsewhere*, and 3) *How Right You Are, Jeeves*. Aristotle said that, because both depend on seeing relations, the ability to laugh is very close to metaphysics. Thus I include here Three More Books of Humor: 1) *The Wodehouse Clergy*, 2) James Thurber, *My Life and Hard Times*, and 3) *The Pocket Book of Ogden Nash*.

The terms "intellectual" and "egg-head" are sometimes used in a pejorative manner. Just because someone is smart does not mean he is wise. Much of the serious disorder in the world can usually be traced back to some intellectual, very often to someone not in our time or in our place or in our tongue. We should remember, however, that the objection to the "intellectual" is not that he uses his brain, but that he uses it wrongly. "Can it be used rightly?" we wonder. One of the greatest intellectual works ever written, Thomas Aquinas's *Summa Theologiae*, was written in the thirteenth century for beginning students, ones about the same age as most undergraduate and graduate students today.

Thomas wrote a brief three-point introduction to the *Summa* explaining to students just why they often found it difficult to learn and to come to a clear knowledge of the truth. The three reasons for the difficulty of learning are: 1) the baffling multiplicity of useless questions and arguments, 2) the things that we want to know are not treated according to the order of the discipline but only according to what is required for explaining some book or dispute, and 3) the frequent repetition of these questions causes confusion and boredom in the minds of the students. Tell me these same points do not hold today! Thomas thought that even the most obscure problem could be spelled out "briefly and lucidly."

Five Books on Thomas Aquinas: 1) Ralph McInerny, *St. Thomas Aquinas*, 2) Josef Pieper, *Guide to St. Thomas Aquinas*, 3) James Weisheipl, *Friar Thomas D'Aquino*, 4) G. K. Chesterton, *St. Thomas Aquinas: The Dumb Ox,* and 5) Brian Davies, *The Thought of Thomas Aquinas*.

We do not "own" truth, however. We can copyright our words, we can register our inventions, but we cannot possess something universal as if it were our private property. The truth will not only "make us free" but it is itself free. We all come in fact to know the same truth, otherwise we could not communicate at all with one another. This is why the modern-day denial of truth is, at the same time, a denial of real human communication and, consequently, in place of truth, an exaltation of power. But if we are helped by others to learn something, of course we ought indeed to be grateful to them.

But for all of us, the truth comes from reality itself, from *what is*. Truth is our judgment about reality. The truth is, as Plato said in *The Republic*, to say of what is, that it is; and to say of what is not, that it is not (477b). This truth, which none of us "owns," is the spiritual bond that potentially unites us to all other members of our human race, as well as with whatever being, including the divine, that is the source of our reasoning powers. From the very fact that we have minds that work the way they do, on their proper objects, we realize that we remain receivers.

The subject matter of our thoughts and the power of thinking itself never come directly from ourselves, from our own creation or choice. In some paradoxical sense, we are gifts to ourselves, endowed with minds sufficiently subtle to realize that we cannot give ourselves such gifts. This is why the great German philosopher Eric Voegelin describes us as beings in search of our "ground," in search of the basis of reality we did not give ourselves. (The best book to become acquainted with Voegelin, incidently, is Ellis Sandoz' *The Voegelinian Revolution*).

Students see in their education and in the culture all too little of the pursuit of truth and of its relation to loving what is good and what is beautiful. However obliquely they are attracted in their souls to something noble, too many students no longer know what it means to be fully civilized or to be virtuous. As Aristotle taught us in his *Ethics*, if we do not have our lives in order, under the rule of right reason, we will simply not see the first principles of reasoning and of living (1095a2-11).

We rarely if ever encounter in universities or in our

culture today attention to the whole, to how things fit together. To find some guide to such fundamental things, we are mostly thrown back on ourselves, on things that are not fashionable to read, on ideas that we find rejected all around us, and mostly, on examination, rejected on untested or contradictory principles.

Not only are the rational and metaphysical sides of our understanding and virtue neglected, but even more we cease to know anything accurate and true about the great revelational tradition. In spite of most of what a student will read on the topic, revelation seeks reason, is addressed to mind and fosters it. The Bible has profound things to tell us, things we clearly ought to know. We now have students in class, even those who have gone to church or synagogue all their lives, who have not the faintest accurate idea about what is said in Scripture, a work that almost every generation before this era has read carefully either to understand or to dispute or to live by.

DO YOU HAVE THIS PROBLEM?

E. F. Schumacher, in *A Guide for the Perplexed*, tells of going to Oxford as a young man, that is, of going to what was thought to be the greatest university of his time. He discovered that what was taught and discussed there bore little meaning and truth to him. Schumacher was forced to look elsewhere for some semblance of an education that dealt with the highest things, that took seriously the great philosophical and religious minds. He already felt issues pressing in his own soul that were never addressed in the great university.[1]

The first and oft-quoted lines of Allan Bloom's disturbingly pertinent book, *The Closing of the American Mind*, began: "There is one thing a professor can be absolutely certain of: almost every student entering the university believes, or says he believes, that truth is relative" (p. 25). That is, unlike the young Schumacher, by the time they reach the universities, most students have already absorbed this dubious doctrine of relativism, the premises of which they have not intellectually examined for their validity. They are simply accepted as if they contained within themselves no contradiction. Contemporary students can assume that their professors in their hearts maintain and carry to further extremes mostly the same contradictory doctrine of relativism. Where does one go when the university and cultural system fail to be good guides and become instead sources of confusion and hindrances to truth?

Five Classic Texts on Philosophy, Good Men, and Death: 1) The *Apology, Crito,* and *Phaedo* of Plato, 2) The account of the death of Christ in the Gospel of *John* (Chapters 13-21) 3) Cicero, *On Duties*, especially Part III, written just before he was executed, 4) Boethius, *The Consolation of Philosophy,* and 5) on Sir Thomas More, Robert Bolt, *Man for All Seasons.*

Before anything can be done, however, the student must become aware that something is profoundly wrong or problematic with the content and spirit of the education he is being given, no matter how famous or how expensive is the university he is attending or has attended. This awareness is by no means an easy thing to come by. It will be looked upon as distinctly odd or wrong-headed by those who have come to accept in their lives such relativist principles. No doubt a young student will soon be in academic trouble if not careful about expressing doubt about university sanctioned public doctrine.

Admitting to oneself that there is a real problem with what one is being given to read, with the methods proposed to substantiate its conclusions, will often take an act of what can only be called intellectual honesty and courage. Many of history's greatest figures—Socrates, Cicero, Christ, Boethius, Thomas More—were not allowed to continue their work in the cities in which they lived; each was eliminated. Yet, they each stood for the truth that was made most graphic to us because they did not compromise or change the standards of mind or God that are the foundations of human well-being and order. Eric Voegelin, in his book on *Plato*, said that after the death of Socrates in Athens, philosophy fled from the city to the Academy. We live in a time evidently when truth is fleeing the Academy. And this is where the intellectually curious student finds himself.

Six Classic Texts Never to Be Left Unread: 1) Plato, *Gorgias*, 2) Aristotle, *Nicomachean Ethics*, 3) Marcus Aurelius, *Meditations*, 4) Augustine, *The Confessions*, 5) Pascal, *Pensées*, and 6) Edmund Burke, *Reflections on the Revolution in France*. There are, of course, many fundamental "classical" texts—*The Republic*, *The City of God*, *The Summa Theologiae*, to name only three.

When a student arrives at a university, he will probably think that what he is about to study will be the best that he can possibly come by. In any university or college—even the worst one—a student can meet new friends, have worthwhile, dignified, and memorable experiences. Many of the unhappiest individuals, however, are those who realize that what is thought to be of the highest prestige and fame is in fact shallow and mostly untrue. They discover that what they are taught or urged to do does not satisfy or ring true. Normally, beginners will have little to alert them to any problems with curriculum, to ideology contained within it, or to what is left out of a program.

Many students have no problem with the educational system or with what they are being taught. There are others, though, who either from their family, religious, or educational background or common-sense experience will begin to detect that all is not well in the academy or in the culture or, for that matter, in one's own soul. While uneasily following, probably for an eventual job, whatever curriculum he has selected or is given, he will nonetheless begin to look about on his own. He needs a certain practical good judgment. At a deeper level, he searches for some way to go; he must, in other words, find "another sort of learning."

What might this other sort of learning be? The first thing to remember is that most great changes, most great encounters with the truth, with what is good, begin in quiet, insignificant places. Oftentimes, small beginnings appear as if by chance, though even chance is subsumed into our calling. So what wakes us up might be what Aristotle called "wonder," a curiosity about what something means or what something is. It might be a love, an awareness that we are not complete in ourselves by ourselves. Even our knowing begins not with knowing ourselves, but with knowing something that is not ourselves, some other thing *that is*.

Some chance story that we read might unsettle us, something of Tolkien, perhaps his essay "On Fairy-Stories," or C. S. Lewis's *Chronicles of Narnia*, or it might be a lecture or conversation, a painting we saw in a gallery. It might even be a class or a classmate that alerts us to something we are missing. Music can do it, both for better and worse. Indeed, following Plato, music today may well be, as Allan Bloom wrote in his chapter in *The Closing of the American Mind*, the real educator of our youth.

Seven Books about Universities: 1) Allan Bloom, *The Closing of the American Mind*, 2) Robert K. Carlson, *Truth on Trial*, 3) Lynne Cheney, *Telling the Truth*, 4) Christopher Derrick, *Escape from Skepticism: Liberal Education as if the Truth Mattered*, 5) Dinesh D'Souza, *Illiberal Education*. No one, however, should miss 6) John Henry Newman, *The Idea of a University*, and 7) Henry Adams, *The Education of Henry Adams*.

What wakes us up might even be an evil, a horror that happened to us or we read about, or something we caused ourselves, something that aroused such perplexity in our souls that we must seek to place it in some kind of order.

Perhaps we ran across the famous definition of evil as the lack of good, of what ought to be there and is not, and wondered what it meant. Indeed, what alerts us could be Shakespeare, now often neglected in the university for ideological reasons. Or it could be the Bible itself, something neglected even more in general academic circles, or it could be curiosity about the overt academic opposition to both.

St. Augustine's famous *Confessions* is a book directed to the very heart of each young person. No other book is quite like it. In it, Augustine excitedly tells us about his reading of Cicero's now lost dialogue, the *Hortensius*. At about the age of nineteen, Augustine's reading of this dialogue in a provincial town in Africa changed his life in the direction of philosophy. Many readers of these words will be themselves nineteen and wonder why they have not had a similarly mind-wrenching experience? At least one reason may be that they have never yet read Augustine or Cicero. By the time we are nineteen, it is indeed time to wake up, as Augustine's example teaches us. I myself remember being in the army at nineteen rather aimlessly wandering through the Post libraries looking for something to read, having little clue (Schall was "clueless"!) about where to begin or how to go about systematically finding some place to start, of finding something that would lead to the truth.

Four Books Once Found in Used Book Stores: 1) J. R. R. Tolkien, *The Silmarillion*, 2) Vivian Mercier, Editor, *Great Irish Short Stories*, 3) Perry Miller, *The American Puritans: Their Prose and Poetry*, and 4) Robert Short, *The Gospel According to Peanuts*.

Cicero lived some five hundred years before Augustine. He himself sent his own son to Greece to study philosophy. Cicero wrote to his son a famous letter, the famous *On Duties*, which attempted to explain to young Marcus how and what to study, a letter that is still worth reading by anyone similarly perplexed. We are all, in this sense, Cicero's sons down the ages. That is to say, what provokes us, incites us, need not come from our own time. Indeed, our own time may be and probably is so disordered that it cannot really alert us to the truth, to *what is*. This is why books from another time are so precious to us and why we need to find them, read them. Someone who knows Aristotle, Plato, Cicero, Augustine, or Aquinas will never be too far from the truth, never out-of-date.

Augustine also recalls his reading by chance a passage of St. Paul's Epistle to the *Romans*. This passage told him that it was time for him to stop his carousing and dickering with life and to change his ways, to direct them toward God in sorrow for all the errors and abuses he had already embraced and committed in his own life. Augustine is an excellent guide for today's students and searchers. He tells them that living their lives in personal moral disorder—often the principal cause of intellectual disorder—will prevent them from seeing the truth. He tells each of us to be honest with ourselves, not to lie to ourselves in our own souls about ourselves, to describe accurately the real results of our choices and deeds, not to be blind to the results of our errors, sins, and defects.

In *Conversations with Eric Voegelin* on a familiar evening in Montreal in 1980, the influential philosopher spoke about contemporary students whose actions belie their theories about themselves. Even though they will claim to be agnostics or relativists, Voegelin observed, they act as if their lives have a purpose, a seriousness that cannot be substantiated by any of their own articulated theories:

> I find that students frequently are flabbergasted, especially those who are agnostics, when I tell them that they all act, whether agnostic or not, as if they were immortal! …They all act as if their lives made sense immortally, even if they deny immortality, deny the existence of a

psyche, deny the existence of a Divinity—in brief, if they are just the sort of fairly corrupt average agnostics that you find among college students today. One shouldn't take their agnosticism too seriously, because in fact they act as if they were not agnostics (p. 6).

What Eric Voegelin was lightly chiding intellectually smug students about in this passage was something that Aristotle long ago taught us; namely, when there is found an inconsistency between our words and our actions, we should, in comparing how we live with what we affirm in public, believe our actions, not our words. Voegelin is also mindful of that most famous passage in the Tenth Book of Aristotle's *Ethics*, in which the Philosopher told us that we

> must not follow those who advise us, being men, to think of human things, and, being mortal, of mortal things, but must, so far as we can, make ourselves immortal, and strain every nerve to live in accordance with the best thing in us; for even if it be small in bulk, much more in power and in worth does it surpass everything. This would seem, too, to be each man himself, since it is the authoritative and better part of him. It would be strange, then, if he were to choose not the life of his self but that of something else (1178a32-b4).

This passage is the great charter of our freedom, freedom from confinement to pedestrian, worldly things that can absorb all our time and energy to leave us none the less empty of even the slightest knowledge of the things that are really important.

WHERE DO I BEGIN?

IN TODAY'S WORLD, when the topic of the defects of university teaching and curricula comes up, the most well-known alternative put forward is the "great books programs." Many universities have such great book programs in one form or another. St. John's College in Annapolis or Santa Fe and Thomas Aquinas College in Santa Paula, California, are probably the best and most famous of these programs, however both would strive to avoid the problem I shall mention. Great books programs have, no doubt, a certain importance. These programs had their modern origin earlier this century at the University of Chicago, conceived of principally by two men of great insight, Mortimer Adler and Robert Hutchins. I take it for granted that we read what are rightly called "great books"— Thucydides, Plato, Aristotle, the Greek tragedians, Cicero,

Marcus Aurelius, the Bible, St. Augustine, some Church fathers, St. Thomas, Shakespeare, and into the moderns.

Frederick D. Wilhelmsen, however, wrote an essay in *Modern Age* entitled "Great Books: Enemies of Wisdom."[2] How on earth could "great books" ever be conceived to be enemies, and not friends, of "wisdom"? Wilhelmsen pointed out, however, what Professor Leo Strauss had also mentioned in his famous essay "What Is Liberal Education?"— that the study of great books can prove to be ambiguous, even intellectually dangerous.[3]

Strauss remarked that we are lucky to be alive during a time when one or two of the great thinkers who ever lived are alive. And if we are alive during their lifetime, we will probably not recognize them. Thus, practically speaking, we encounter the greatest minds among those no longer alive, and the way we encounter such minds is to read their books carefully—which today often means taking a common-sense stand on those contemporary theories that tell us we can find no truth in a text. The very existence of the great books enables us to escape from any tyranny of the present, from the idea that we only want to study what is currently "relevant" or immediately useful. This access to noble minds is surely a great legacy and capacity that we have been given.

Strauss also mentioned, however—which is also Wilhelmsen's point—that careful study of the great thinkers reveals eventually that they contradict each other. And contradictories cannot both be right; but they can stimulate our curiosity. The study of "great books" can lead students to a kind of implicit relativism or to a choice of a great mind that leads them far afield. Or they will think that if the great thinkers do not agree, "who am I to dispute them?" "Why bother?" The whole point of this present essay, while in no way doubting Strauss's point about the great minds contradicting each other, is to suggest that this controversy among the great minds can lead to a false sort of humility, something that misunderstands what the mind is about. In the modern world, Chesterton said, humility is misplaced; it is thought to be located in the intellect where it does not belong, whereas it is a virtue of the will, an awareness of our own tendencies to pride. We should not doubt our minds but our motives. The condition of not knowing should not lead us to a further skepticism but to a more intense search for truth. We should see in what sense a great mind might reveal something of the truth even in its error.

The best place to begin for any young man or woman

today can be stated in two steps: 1) the step of self-discipline and 2) the step of a personal library; both of these together will yield that freedom which is necessary to escape academic dreariness and to discover the wonder of reality, of *what is*. Even at its best, of course, learning means we need a lot of help, even grace, but we are here talking about what we can do ourselves.

SELF-DISCIPLINE

The first step in a plan to advance on the pursuit of truth begins by recalling what I noted about Lee at the outset, namely, that a sense of self-denial must be developed so that we can do our duty, what we ought. The notion of self-denial or more properly of self-discipline is never an especially pleasant one. I would never pretend that it is. However, a minimum insight into ourselves teaches us that we are all in some sense fallen beings, to recall *Genesis*. Almost always, on reflection upon ourselves, we can find something in us, in our desires or habits or choices, that would prevent us from confronting the really important things.

Josef Pieper, in his *Anthology*, recalls Thomas Aquinas's discussion of the vice of sloth—*acedia*, in Latin. Is this such an unfamiliar vice? It does not mean just laziness, but a lethargy that prevents us from making the effort to look at what is really important in our lives or from taking any positive step that might make us aware of what we should know or do. Some experience of students over the years will make any perceptive teacher acutely aware that the major cause of students' failure to learn anything in a class is related, on their part, to a lack of self-discipline, to their inability or unwillingness to rule their day, to decide what is important, how much time it will take, and then actually to do what needs to be done.

Five Books by Josef Pieper: 1) *'Divine Madness': Plato's Case against Secular Humanism*, 2) *The Four Cardinal Virtues*, 3) *In Tune with the World: A Theory of Festivity*, 4) *Living the Truth*, which includes, *The Truth of All Things* and *Reality and the Good,* and 5) everyone should read *Leisure: The Basis of Culture.*

Clearly, the notion of discipline, especially disciplining one's own self, has to do with the systematic process by which we acquire knowledge or virtue or art. Discipline means instruction, especially organized instruction. When we add the notion of "self" to this instruction, we are indicating that we are ourselves objects of our own rule, of our own need to instruct ourselves.

Ultimately, no one else can do this ordering for us.

Our lives are ours to order according to some sort of principle or purpose. Our lives are also ours to leave in disorder or in an order that deviates from what it is we know we ought to be or do. We should not, moreover, underestimate the difficulty we confront in ruling ourselves. Christianity even suggests that most of us might need something more than ourselves properly to see and rule ourselves, some grace and some instruction.

This topic of ordering our lives according to some principle is really what the First Book of Aristotle's *Ethics* is about. We are to look back reflectively on our deeds and our thoughts and see, if we can, that for which we act, that which we think to be most important, and that which governs all we do. No doubt we can mislead ourselves in this self-reflection. We can think we act for the noblest purposes, whereas in fact, as all our friends know, we act for money or pleasure or vain honors. It is difficult to see ourselves as we are, even if this inner "seeing" is one of the most important things we must do for ourselves. The famous Delphic admonition, "know thyself," meant at least this honest inner-knowledge of our own implicit ends, in addition to knowing the kind of being we are by nature—our human being, something we did not give ourselves.

The student who first comes to the university is no doubt exhilarated by a kind of new-found freedom. He is still too young, as Aristotle had already intimated in the First Book of his *Ethics*, really to have acquired a good knowledge of himself or a firm capacity to rule himself. He will have many bad habits—too much time at television, at running about, at sundry forms of dissipation with which all high school and college students are familiar. Many young men and women no doubt have by the time they reach college already failed to discipline themselves. They have barely begun to acquire the habits and incentives necessary to figure out, not what they should do in terms of a profession or job, but what life itself is about—itself a lifetime task, to be sure. Many, unfortunately, make very serious mistakes early in life. College is a place in which, if we are wise, these mistakes can be corrected or, on the contrary, if we are not so wise, magnified indefinitely.

Self-discipline, the rule over all of our given passions, fears, dreams, thoughts, can be, if simply taken for itself, a dangerous thing. We can be Stoics who conceive self-discipline somehow as an end in itself, whereas it is really the prerequisite for seeing and loving what is not ourselves. Self-discipline can become a form of pride in which we attribute to ourselves complete mastery over ourselves with no willingness to guide ourselves to ends that are to be served or people who are to be loved. Nonetheless, our "bare" selves are objects to ourselves. We recognize that our ability to accomplish anything at all begins with some realization that we must take control of ourselves. We must begin to note in ourselves those things that cause us troubles. These difficulties can be other students, perhaps even teachers—anyone, in short, who interferes with our studies or with our responsibilities, including our responsibilities to God. What impedes us can be things like drink or drugs or television or parties or work or our own laziness or an *eros* untempered by any sense of justice, friendship, duty, purpose, or permanence.

The object of self-discipline in the best sense then is not ourselves. That probably sounds strange. The classical writers, I think, used to relate self-discipline to liberty. The person who was most free was the one who had the most control over himself. The person who was most unfree was the one who was ruled by pleasures, money, or power. Self-discipline does not, however, solve the question of what is knowledge or truth or good; self-discipline is a means, not an end in itself. It is like being all dressed up with no place to go. In this sense, it is instrumental, something good for the sake of something else. The current Pontiff, Pope John Paul II, put it well in his book, *Crossing the Threshold of Hope*: "the fundamental dimension of man's existence...is always a co-existence."

We are ourselves, to be sure, and we are to rule ourselves. But once we have managed to approach this no doubt difficult issue, what remains is the rest of our lives. We can then begin to focus on the things of the highest importance and dignity, something we would be unable to do if we did not succeed in imposing some self-discipline on ourselves. There is an intimate connection between our moral life and our intellectual life. Sometimes I think the history of our times can be described as an argument about whether or not this connection is true. Self-discipline is the beginning of wisdom, not its end. When we have discovered the purpose for which self-discipline exists, we will, if we are sane, hardly recall anything about self-discipline because it has enabled us to become free to see and do so much else.

The second step, if I can call it that, to advancement in the pursuit of objective truth has to do with a personal library. Modern computers provide many materials instantaneously in a short, handy form on disc or on-line. Indeed, the amount and variety of material available through the computer is so enormous that we cannot easily comprehend its reach. We are profoundly fortunate to have almost the whole of the world's books, music, art, journals, and press available to us through something like Internet or the World Wide Web. Nonetheless, the most important ideas and concepts still appear first in the print media, in books. "How to read a book," to use Mortimer Adler's famous phrase, is still one of the most importantskills we can develop in our pursuit of the truth.

But we don't have to read everything. One can be well on his way to what I am trying to encourage by reading a very few books, and these not necessarily large ones or even famous ones. The things that I suggest here, then, are not necessarily the "great books" which I take it that most of us have some knowledge of. These should be read and reread. I remain a firm believer in C. S. Lewis's famous observation that we have not read a great book at all if we have read it only once.

Six Books Given to Me as a Gift and Now in My Personal Library: 1) Ray Bradbury, *Dandelion Wine*, 2) Gilbert Highet, *Poets in a Landscape*, 3) Thomas Mann, *Stories and Episodes*, 4) G. K. Chesterton, *The Defendant*, 5) Thornton Wilder, *The Eighth Day*, and 6) *The Letters of Evelyn Waugh*.

Anyone who has any curiosity at all will have some books and articles lying about. Nothing is more unnerving than to go into a house or apartment and to notice there not a single book or journal of any significance. On the other hand, it used to be said of the Americans on the frontier that they only had two books that they could carry along with them. These were the Bible and Shakespeare. The fact is that at some fundamental level most of the important things about human life were contained in these two books. No library on this new frontier that we are on in modern academia should lack either of these books. They can usually be found or purchased for a relatively small cost. The philosopher Eric Voegelin, a German, read the complete works of Shakespeare each year, an impressive accomplishment. And if neither of these books is mentioned by our professors or appear in our academic curriculum, do not conclude that there is something wrong with either of these two books.

So what do I mean by our own personal library? I know that most of us cannot help but accumulate reams of paper in the form of books, articles, journals, letters. A. D. Sertillanges' *The Intellectual Life* remains a good guide to how to take notes, to classify what we have read, to select. His suggestions can easily be translated into our computer files. When we move or build, we should look for places to keep our collected books and printed matter. Read books are a precious item. No one else will ever read a book quite the same way that we do. Books can speak in many different ways, even at different times in our own lives. I always assign what I consider fine and great books to my students, books that are worth reading again and again. I would be ashamed to assign to a student a book that I did not think worth keeping. I have myself read Aristotle and Plato and Aquinas and Chesterton many, many times—finding something new in each reading. Furthermore, at differing times of my life I have seen things in these works that I could not have seen when I was younger.

Five Books by G. K. Chesterton and Two by His Friend Hilaire Belloc—each of these men wrote over a hundred books and thousands of essays, none of which I have ever found boring or from which I did not learn something of great value: by Chesterton, 1) *Orthodoxy*,

2) *What's Wrong with the World,* 3) *Charles Dickens,* 4) *The Everlasting Man,* and 5) *The Autobiography;* by Belloc, 1) *The Path to Rome* and 2) *The Four Men,* both of Belloc's books are walks, one through France and Italy, the other through Sussex in England. There is a journal called *The Chesterton Review,* now distributed by ISI, that is always worth a look.

Thus, I conceive a personal library to be composed of books we have read again. I always tell my students that I expect them to keep the books I assign them for the rest of their lives. I also encourage students to bring their books to tests. I consider a book that we have read to be part of our memory, something we can quickly go back to, something we can look at again when a problem or controversy arises. Often we know that we have read the precise argument we need.

Frequently, in some discussion, we realize that we did not make a good argument or remember an exact citation. There is nothing wrong with going back and in our leisure finding out what we had forgotten or not placed in the right context. The trouble with arguments, Chesterton said, is that we never have enough time to complete them, that short arguments are almost always unfair arguments. Our personal libraries, our chosen few read books, will enable us to think things through.

Six Memorable Novels, among the Millions: 1) Jane Austen, *Emma*, 2) Sigrid Undset, *Kristin Lavransdatter*, 3) Wendell Berry, *The Memory of Old Jack*, 4) Willa Cather, *Death Comes to the Archbishop*, and 5) Walker Percy, *Lancelot*. Everyone should read at one point in his life Dostoyevsky's 6) *The Brothers Karamazov*.

In this personal library of ours, as I have explained, we ought to have books that we have read, though there is nothing wrong with accumulating in advance books we might never read or read only years later. No serious book-lover will ever die having read every book he has managed to collect. This is not a sign of dilatoriness but of eagerness, anticipation. I do not mean here the technical books of a given discipline that quickly become out-of-date, though even these preserve a certain history. Rather, I mean those books which explain things, that touch on the truths of our being, that reach to *what is*.

Very rarely will we read a sane book that does not lead us to someone else, to some other topic or writer we did not know about, but whom we are now incited to read. Problems that we could not quite fathom when we were nineteen or thirty or forty, and thus left quietly churning in our memories, can suddenly become clear when we read something at fifty or sixty.

Three great books on love, for example—a topic of the most difficulty to find adequate guidance—are, 1) C. S. Lewis's *The Four Loves*, 2) Josef Pieper's *About Love*, and 3) Denis de Rougemont's *Love in the Western World*. I had read C. S. Lewis years ago. I found Pieper in a library in Los Gatos, California. I had never heard of de Rougemont's book for much of my life. One day a Mexican graduate student in one of my classes, sort of sizing me up, I guess, came into my office and gave me a copy of the de Rougemont book. He said simply, "I think you will like it." It was one of the most wonderful of books. I keep it handy and realize that Pieper and Lewis and de Rougemont complement each other on this most splendid and delicate of human and divine topics.

ON TEACHERS AND TEACHING

THE CENTRAL CHAPTER in *Another Sort of Learning* was entitled "What A Student Owes His Teacher." Students often have told me that they had never thought of the idea that they "owe" something to their teachers; to wit, their interest, their study habits, their good will, their diligence, their very capacity to learn something they do not already know. Yet, it is so; such things are "owed" if, alas as is not always the case, the teacher is himself inspired by and seeks to pass along the highest things, the things that are worth learning, some knowledge of *what is*, of reality itself. Students can, no doubt, often understand the "justice" argument. They themselves or their parents have to pay a hefty sum in taxes or in income for them even to be in college. Their failure to learn is an act of injustice to their parents. But the kind of "owing" I have in mind here reaches to issues of honor, of integrity, and above all, to the effort it takes to know the truth for its own sake. This latter effort is really what the student "owes," even to those who are paying his way through college.

Thus, as both Plato and Aristotle remarked, we love Homer, we love Socrates (four names everyone should know), but we love truth more. We need to be taught, but we may not encounter a good or truth-seeking teacher. We may have to find what is true or good or right in obscure books that no one has yet told us about.

In his *Guide to Thomas Aquinas*, Josef Pieper stated the following about teaching and teachers:

Teaching does not consist in a man's making public talks on the results of his meditations, even if he does so *ex cathedra* before a large audience. Teaching in the real sense takes place only when the hearer is reached—not by dint of some personal magnetism or verbal magic, but rather, when the truth of what is said reaches the hearer as truth. Real teaching takes place only when its ultimate result—which must be intended from the start—is achieved—when the hearer is "taught".... Being taught means to perceive that what the teacher has said is true and valid, and to perceive why it is so. Teaching therefore presupposes that the hearer is sought out where he is to be found. Thus teaching implies proceeding from the existing position and disposition of the hearer.... The teacher, then, must proceed from what is valid in the opinion of the hearer to the fuller and purer truth as he, the teacher, understands it (pp. 32-33).

Teaching means, Thomas Aquinas said, the "handing over" of what one learns and contemplates to others, *contemplata aliis tradere*. We want the truth to be known, to be what we hold. Plato warned us about having a "lie" in our own souls about reality, a lie that we knowingly choose for ourselves. We do not want to deceive ourselves about the most important things.[4]

Four Older but Insightful Books on How to Prepare for an Intellectual Life: 1) A. D. Sertillanges, *The Intellectual Life*, 2) Mortimer Adler, *How to Read a Book*, 3) Gilbert Highet, *The Art of Teaching*, and 4) Jacques Barzun, *The Teacher in America*.

In speaking about *teaching*, I want to emphasize what a teacher owes his students, as I think it helpful in understanding what a student owes his teacher. I am most thankful to students over the years for the continued opportunity they give me for reading and re-reading so many things. But to begin reading at all, a student must read a book for the first time. This is what I have tried to do for students in insisting that they come to class regularly, after having carefully read the text. The student who does not do this work himself is unteachable. No teacher can really help him.

Some books, no doubt, take all our lives to understand. Plato was very late in coming to my own purview. This is not a defect either in the book or in the student or in the teacher. Rather it is an acknowledgment of the profundity of what we are and where we are. Most students are the age of Plato's potential philosophers, those young citizens of Athens whom Socrates was accused of corrupting. But their undisciplined souls, as Socrates also knew, were being drawn one way and the other by the attractions of a thousand fascinating and often disrupting things, not at all unlike students of any generation. Plato, in the Eighth Book of *The Republic*, moreover warned students against those insecure professors who seek to imitate their students in thought, speech, and dress, in habit of mind, as if these professors had learned nothing themselves and stood for nothing except the latest fad. So while being a student requires some trust, it also requires a kind of Augustinian realism, an awareness that students in their early twenties are not yet likely to possess much real human experience.

Let me also recall Samuel Johnson, whose famous biography by his devotee Boswell is, I think, something along with the Bible that you should read a bit every day, if only for the delight of it. At least this is what I do. Johnson had a young friend who must have been more or less the age of most students, again a man who reminds us of Plato's potential philosophers, as Johnson himself reminds us of Socrates. This young man was named Bennett Langton, from a famous English family that once included, during the reign of King John, a Cardinal of the Roman Church. In 1757, Langton was a student at Trinity College in Oxford. Johnson had occasion to write to him about the general relation of knowledge to life. Let me cite these lines from Samuel Johnson. They are ones any student can take away with him either for testing the truth that he may have learned in his college or for finding it elsewhere, if he succeeded in learning little truth in his academic career.

"I know not any thing more pleasant, or more instructive, than to compare experience with expectation, or to register from time to time the difference between ideas and reality," Johnson wrote to this young student.

> It is by this kind of observation that we grow daily less liable to be disappointed. You, who are very capable of anticipating futurity, and raising phantoms before your own eyes, must often have imagined to yourself an academical life, and have conceived what would be the manners, the views, and the conversation, of men devoted to letters; how they would choose their companions, how they would direct their studies, and how they would regulate their lives. Let me know what you have expected and what you have found (*Boswell's Life of Johnson*, I, p. 224).

Note what is said here. Ideas need to be tested by reality, by *what is*. If our ideas are not so tested, we will easily find life a disappointment, filled with phantoms of our own making. Yet, as Socrates and Christ taught us in considering their deaths, reality too needs its testing.

While we are young, as Johnson quaintly put it, we can "anticipate futurity" and easily "raise phantoms before (our) eyes." The "academical life" has many imaginings. Doubt it not. We are asked, furthermore, to report back to Johnson, to the philosopher/teacher, what we have found, how our experiences have shown the limits of our expectations, not to the detriment of experience, but to the moderation of our own phantoms, our own untested ideas and musings.

For a professor, there is nothing more noble than to let him, or someone down the ages, in some letter, essay, or book, perhaps, know what was the difference between what his student expected and what he experienced. This is, after all, in part why we have friends, to recall a section in Aristotle (Books 8 and 9 of *The Ethics*) that all students invariably and not surprisingly love.[5] A good teacher addresses his students carefully: "Do not be disappointed with life unless you are the cause of the disappointment." I have tried, however, to suggest that joy is more profound than sadness. We begin our intellectual lives not with need, nor less with desire, but with wonder and enchantment. A student and a teacher read together many books that they might otherwise have missed. Both need to make efforts to know the truth of things, the ordinary things and the highest things, that the one and the other might have overlooked had they not had time, serious time, together.

It is any honorable professor's hope that his students will come to realize that their minds are, as E. F. Schumacher said in his *Guide for the Perplexed*, "adequate" to know *all that is*. And I would add the hope that students will acquire something of that driven enthusiasm of the young Augustine to pursue the truth of things, even unto the City of God.

WHERE DO I FIND TIME FOR ALL THIS LIBERAL LEARNING?

❧

THE LEARNING THAT is here described is called "liberal," that is, freeing. It takes a lot of work to be free. Yet, we need some way to become what we are. No one can do this for us, but we cannot do it merely by ourselves either. We need guides to find guides. Something that Aristotle once said should be reiterated here; namely, that many people who do not know books are nevertheless very wise, often wiser than the so-called learned. Perhaps it will be our grandfather or an ordinary farmer or worker. We should look for and respect the experience of ordinary people. Wherever there is a mind and reality, someone can find the truth. This in no way lessens our drive to know more completely and to seek the guidance of good books, good teachers, good parents, good libraries, good friends.

Does this effort to find good intellectual guidance mean that we have to check out of school or office and hole up in our own private libraries, become recluses? Perhaps for some few it will mean this. The monastic or contemplative life does exist in many forms. However, as A. D. Sertillanges said in *The Intellectual Life*, each of us can manage to find some time each day, each week to read and reflect. Using a few odd hours in his week, a friend of mine has managed to write a book on the Churches of Rome, translate Thomas à Kempis's *Imitation of Christ*, and, now he tells me, do a commentary on Dante.

The famous author of western stories, Louis L'Amour, wrote a very marvelous memoir called *The Education of a Wandering Man*. No book is better than this one for telling us how to find the time we need to read in an already busy life. Find this book and see how much good sense L'Amour makes about using the time we have riding on buses, in the odd moments of our day, to read. L'Amour made lists of the books he read each year.

Evelyn Waugh's biography is called *A Little Learning*, a title with obvious reminders of the famous phrase from Alexander Pope that "a little learning is a dangerous thing." Waugh is always worth reading. His description of the education of Hooper at the beginning of his acclaimed novel *Brideshead Revisited* is almost prophetic as to the condition of the education most of us are now subject to. Let me cite these memorable lines from Waugh, principally to serve as an examination of our own intellectual consciences:

> Hooper was no romantic. He had not as a child ridden with Rupert's horse or sat among the camp fires at Xanthus-side; at the age when my eyes were dry to all save poetry—that stoic, red-skin interlude which our schools introduce between the fast flowing tears of the child and the man—Hooper had wept often, but never for Henry's speech on St. Crispin's Day, nor for the epitaph at Thermopylae. The history they taught him had few battles in it but, instead, a profusion of detail about humane legislation and recent industrial change.

Gallipoli, Balaclava, Quebec, Lepanto, Bannockburn, Roncevales, and Marathon—these, and the Battle in the West where Arthur fell, and a hundred such names whose trumpet-notes, even now in my sere and lawless state, called to me irresistibly across the intervening years with all the clarity and strength of boyhood, sounded in vain to Hooper (p. 9).

Any student can test his current education by these lines, I think, to see if he has had it any better than poor Hooper.

We don't, then, have to switch schools or curriculum to set our minds in the right direction. One such chance passage from Waugh or Lewis could do it. In fact, the morning that I wrote these lines I came across the following passage from Samuel Johnson written in 1779. Notice how the word "learning" is used in this very passage: "I [Johnson] am always for getting a boy forward in his learning; for that is a sure good. I would let him at first read *any* English book which happens to engage his attention; because you have done a great deal when you have brought him to have entertainment from a book. He'll get better books afterwards" (II, p. 290). The two key ideas are already here—get him started, get him to better books. But above all, get his attention, his engagement.

This sentiment was introduced to me in a class I took with a famous professor by the name of Rudolf Allers. I remember him saying in class one day that we should always be reading novels, even bad novels; for in their particularity, we will always find something, some incident, some character, some chance insight, that will teach us something we could have learned nowhere else. Allers's own book, *The Psychology of Character*, is still worth reading.

Consequently, I often think these reflections, this guide to liberal learning, ought to bear a sort of saucy subtitle like, "How to Get an Education Even While Still in College." We cannot really escape from the kinds of schools, media, and culture that are all around us by going someplace else. But we can, if we attend to it, realize that something is wrong, something more needs to be said, and that we have to search out alternatives to ourselves. The alternative we want is one that leads us to truth and wisdom, to right order and virtue, that leads us to ask where even these things lead us. Such things do not come automatically. We have to do our part. I intend these suggestions of books and ideas to be that alternative.

Where do we find the time? We find it in the lives we

lead. As Louis L'Amour says, time enough is always there. If we look at what we do, the time we lose on television or dithering about a hundred other things, we can with some enterprise find that little learning which is not a dangerous but a liberating thing. "Where would I begin?" someone might ask. I remember in high school having read with delight James Oliver Curwood's dog stories and my father's copy of Robert Hugh Benson's *The Lord of the World*, books I now think in retrospect fulfilled Johnson's wise suggestion to let a young person read any English book that would "engage his attention."

I also remember having found in some library a book by Aldous Huxley and another by Josef Stalin. I thought both were interesting books, but was again "clueless," that great word, about what they really were about. So it often takes us a long time to find a good guide and have enough sense to read a Huxley and a Stalin critically. In brief, *remember Hooper*, into whom we all can turn if our souls are not moved by *what is*.

Thus, I presume that anyone who reads these lines will have already begun something, somewhere. He will have a little learning. He will be in danger. He will have gone into some vast library and wondered where to begin. He will have gone to class and, perhaps like Schumacher at Oxford, have realized that what is presented there is all pretty irrelevant to, if not corruptive of, the important things. So, to put myself in the place of the student or ex-student to whom these lines are addressed, I would begin by finding some used book store, taking some time to find a book that might happen to appear on "Schall's Unlikely List" and begin. Schumacher, Chesterton, L'Amour, Bochenski, Lewis, Pieper, or Dorothy Sayers, even her mystery novels, would be fine. Any of these books will, I think, provoke; will, on reflection, be one of the better books that we later find after we have begun to read the others. We need some self-discipline, our own personal library where we keep what we read, and we need good guides. I leave these reflections with a final remark of Chesterton, who once said, I forget where, that there is no such thing as a boring subject, only bored people. This brief guide, if it does nothing else, will, I hope, prevent us from falling into that *acedia*, that sloth, that deters us from really finding what truth and reality are about. This latter quest is, after all, the great human adventure.

James V. Schall, S.J.

NOTES:

1. On this famous passage see Schumacher's remarks in his *A Guide for the Perplexed*, p. 3, wherein he cites the same passage from Thomas Aquinas's *Commentary* on the *Ethics* of Aristotle.

2. Frederick D. Wilhelmsen, "Great Books: Enemies of Wisdom," *Modern Age*, (Summer /Fall, 1987), 321-31. Since I have mentioned Professor Wilhelmsen, let me list four of his books that any student would profit by: 1) *Man's Knowledge of Reality*, 2) *The Metaphysics of Love*, 3) *The Paradoxical Structure of Existence*, and 4) *From My Pen and Podium* (each of these Wilhelmsen books are available from PCP—Preserving Christian Publications—at 315-942-6339).

   Mention of *Modern Age*, likewise, leads me to recall here five journals that are worth looking at. These are literary, intellectual quarterly journals that not many people will know about: *Humanitas, Academic Questions, Faith & Reason, The Review of Politics*, and *The Intercollegiate Review*. Subscriptions to *The Intercollegiate Review* and *Modern Age* can be obtained through their publishers, the Intercollegiate Studies Institute (also the publisher of this guide).

3. Leo Strauss, *Liberalism: Ancient and Modern*. Leo Strauss is himself one of the very best writers about contemporary thought. He is difficult to read and requires much attention, but he is worth every effort. Here are four books by Strauss that are worth knowing about: 1) *City and Man*, 2) *Natural Right and History*, 3) *What Is Political Philosophy?*, and 4) *The Rebirth of Classical Political Rationalism: An Introduction to the Thought of Leo Strauss*. I also recommend Susan Orr's *Jerusalem and Athens: Reason and Revelation in the Works of Leo Strauss*.

4. A most excellent brief statement on "The Teacher" is found in Yves Simon's fundamental book, *A General Theory of Authority*, pp. 94-100. The discussions of friendship, truth, and doing good in this book are of exceptional worth.

5. See my essay, "Aristotle on Friendship," *The Classical Bulletin*, 65 (#3 & 4, 1989), 83-88. Nothing surprises students more than to find out that Aristotle describes quite accurately what is often their most burning questions. See also on this topic Chapter 8, "Unknown to the Ancients: God and Friendship," in my *What Is God Like?*

APPENDIX:
SCHALL'S UNLIKELY LIST OF BOOKS TO KEEP SANE BY

❧

EACH OF THESE BOOKS, I think, shows a certain profundity, a certain brevity, a certain charm. I have included books on play, on philosophy, on resources, on authority, on just about everything, including the seven deadly sins! Yet another book is on food, one on science, some essays, some theology, some history, some conversation.

1) *Josef Pieper—an Anthology*
2) G. K. Chesterton, *Orthodoxy*
3) J. M. Bochenski, *Philosophy—an Introduction*
4) Dorothy Sayers, *The Whimsical Christian*
5) E. F. Schumacher, *A Guide for the Perplexed*
6) Yves Simon, *A General Theory of Authority*
7) Eric Mascall, *The Christian Universe*
8) Flannery O'Connor, *The Habit of Being: The Letters of Flannery O'Connor*
9) Hilaire Belloc, *Selected Essays*

10) C. S. Lewis, *The Abolition of Man*

11) John Paul II, *Crossing the Threshold of Hope*

12) Peter Kreeft, *Back to Virtue*

13) Johann Huizinga, *Homo Ludens*

14) *Conversations with Walker Percy*

15) Henry Fairlie, *The Seven Deadly Sins Today*

16) Stanley Jaki, *The Road of Science and the Ways to God*

17) *Conversations with Eric Voegelin*

18) Herbert Butterfield, *Christianity and History*

19) Henry Veatch, *Rational Man*

20) Leon Kass, *The Hungry Soul*

EMBARKING ON A LIFELONG PURSUIT OF KNOWLEDGE?

*Take Advantage of These New Resources
& a New Website*

❧

The ISI Guides to the Major Disciplines are part of the Intercollegiate Studies Institute's (ISI) **Student Self-Reliance Project**, an integrated, sequential program of educational supplements designed to guide students in making key decisions that will enable them to acquire an appreciation of the accomplishments of Western civilization.

Developed with fifteen months of detailed advice from college professors and students, these resources provide advice in course selection and guidance in actual coursework. The Project elements can be used independently by students to navigate the existing university curriculum in a way that deepens their understanding of our Western intellectual heritage. As indicated below, the Project's integrated components will answer key questions at each stage of a student's education.

What are the strengths and weaknesses of the most selective schools?
Choosing the Right College directs prospective college students to the best and worst that top American colleges have to offer.

What is the essence of a liberal arts education?
A Student's Guide to Liberal Learning will introduce students to the vital connection between liberal education and political liberty.

What core courses should every student take?
A Core Curriculum Self-Study Guide will instruct students how to build their own core curriculum, utilizing electives available at virtually every university, and how to identify and overcome contemporary political biases in those courses.

How can students learn from the best minds in their major field of study?
Study Guides to the Major Disciplines will introduce students to overlooked and misrepresented classics, facilitating work within their majors. Guides currently in production assess the fields of literature, political philosophy, European and American history, and economics.

Which great modern thinkers are neglected?
The Library of Modern Thinkers will introduce students to great minds who have contributed to the literature of the West and who are neglected or denigrated in today's classroom. Figures who make up this series include Robert Nisbet, Eric Voegelin, Wilhelm Roepke, Ludwig von Mises, Will Herberg, and many more.

In order to address the academic problems faced by every student in an ongoing manner, a new website, **www.collegeguide.org**, was recently launched. It offers easy access to unparalleled resources for making the most of one's college experience—and it features an interactive component that will allow students to pose questions about academic life on America's college campuses.

These features make ISI a one-stop organization for serious students of all ages. Visit **www.isi.org** or call **1-800-526-7022** and consider adding your name to the 50,000-plus ISI membership list of teachers, students, and professors.